# PROPLINERS

Clinton H. Groves

Motorbooks International
Publishers & Wholesalers

First published in 1994 by Motorbooks International
Publishers & Wholesalers, PO Box 2, 729 Prospect
Avenue, Osceola, WI 54020 USA

Motorbooks International is a certified trademark,
registered with the United States Patent Office

The information in this book is true and
complete to the best of our knowledge. All
recommendations are made without any guarantee on
the part of the author or Publisher, who also disclaim
any liability incurred in connection with the use of this
data or specific details

We recognize that some words, model names and
designations, for example, mentioned herein are the
property of the trademark holder. We use them for
identification purposes only. This is not an official
publication

Motorbooks International books are also available at
discounts in bulk quantity for industrial or sales-
promotional use. For details write to Special Sales
Manager at the Publisher's address

Library of Congress Cataloging-in-Publication Data

Groves, Clinton.
    Propliners / Clinton H. Groves.
       p.  cm. — (Enthusiast color series)
    Includes index.
    ISBN 0-87938-866-8
    1. Transport planes—History.  2. Transport
planes—Miscellanea.  I. Title.  II. Series.
    TL685.7.G773       1994
    629.133'343—dc20        93-48649

**On the front cover:** Converted to freighter status, this
American DC-7 lands at Oakland in the spring of 1962.
*William T. Larkins*

**On the frontispiece:** A Transocean Stratocruiser in the
airline's final days. With Stratocruisers and Connies to
compete against 707s and DC-8s, Transocean ran out of
operating capital and shut down. *Lawrence S. Smalley*

**On the title page:** An Ozark Convair 240 that the airline
bought from a European carrier. The Convairs didn't
stay long, as Martin 4-0-4s from Mohawk replaced
them. *Lawrence S. Smalley*

**On the back cover:** Shown here in United colors, the
Stratocruiser was the largest piston-powered airliner in
scheduled service anywhere. *William T. Larkins*

Printed and bound in Hong Kong

# Contents

# Dedication

The *American Heritage Dictionary* defines mentor as "a wise and trusted counselor or teacher." Eastern Air Lines Captain William E. Helm, the son of my next-door neighbor in Louisville, Kentucky, may not have realized he was my mentor. Born 16 January 1923, Bill completed his Army Air Corps B-17 pilot training in Roswell, New Mexico, on 15 January 1943, the day I was born. A week later, he visited his parents and my mother gave him my baby picture. After he reached his duty station in England, he taped that picture to the instrument panel glare shield of his B-17. Bill said it was his good luck charm; he was able to complete his twenty-five missions.

After the war Eastern Air Lines hired Bill as a pilot. Based at Newark, he often bid Louisville flights so he could visit his mother and father. His parents would ask me if I wanted to go to Standiford Field (SDF) when Bill was flying in. He always had time to answer my questions and take me on a walkaround of his airplane. In those days, his aircraft was a Lockheed L-188 Electra, later a Boeing 720-025. I am sure Bill had no idea just how much his attention and willingness to talk meant to me. I thought he looked like John Wayne. With a scar under one eyebrow that made that part of the eyebrow white before the rest of his hair, Bill's appearance was quite distinctive.

Like Bill, I graduated from the Spartan School of Aeronautics in Tulsa. I always wanted to work for Eastern but had to settle for TWA. Bill retired before Eastern's troubles and died 4 December 1989. He did not have to go through the bitter labor strife or the eventual demise of Eastern. I find comfort in that. Thank you, Bill Helm, for all you did.

# Introduction

**17** December 2003 marks the 100-year anniversary of powered flight. We've come a long way in that time. This book will try to take you back to those early days, from a time when flying really was dangerous, through and beyond the times that the Douglas, Martin, Boeing and Lockheed piston-powered giants were in their prime. As this is a color photo essay, the photos of the old airplanes are of restored aircraft. Kodachrome color slide film became available to the public around 1937. With an exposure index of only 10 and the best 35mm camera of the day being an Argus C3 with an f3.5 lens, daylight photography required the use of a tripod. The photo arrangement herein, except for the last chapter, is chronologically by first flight date. The slides will usually show the airframes as they appeared a few years later with more modern paint schemes and/or weather radar added.

For those who never experienced this era I regret that there are no words to adequately describe the smells, sounds, and sensations of flying with radial engines, oil leaks, volatile high octane aviation fuels, massive three- or four-blade propellers, and handwritten tickets. The age was as different in the air as it was on the ground where coal-fired steam locomotives belched black smoke and steam and railroad waiting rooms were filled with cigar smoke.

I obtained many of the slides used in this book when I purchased the working collection of Thompson Productions of Beecher, Illinois. I obtained others through trades or outright purchase. Collecting these images has not been an easy task; people just don't want to give up their slides. The TWA DC-3 shot cost me $500, and I obtained it only after two years of begging and raising my offer.

With my loss of ramp access to the San Francisco International Airport ramp, I have done little original photography since 1982. The exception is Honolulu, where I try to shoot at least twice a year. Michael A. Sparkman, a friend from Huntsville, Alabama, did most of the data research while I did the photo work.

If you wish, you may purchase the 35mm duplicate slides in this book and more from the Airliners America/ATP color slide catalog offered by Motorbooks International/ Zenith Aviation (item number 111239). Add them to your vacation slides or edit them into your video conversions of old 8mm home movies.

So many people have given so much for what we take for granted today. Time brings the cruel fate of becoming lost in history and insignificant to new generations, most of whom just don't care about the lives lost building the commercial airway systems that circle our globe. Now you have the opportunity to learn a little about our early aircraft. Find a comfortable chair, your best reading glasses, and a cool beverage. Sit back and enjoy the photos and stories. Enter a mood perhaps best described in the song written by M. Hamlisch, A. Bergman, and M. Bergman, as sung by Barbra Streisand, "Misty watercolor memories of the way we were."

Four decades ago: A huge crowd has assembled and several aircraft have been rolled into place for the dedication of the San Francisco International Airport terminal on 28 August 1954. *Lawrence S. Smalley*

# Chapter 1

# From Wood to Metal

We've come a long way since 1903. Today, airline passengers think they have a problem if their individual video monitor or powered air vent doesn't work. In the earliest days of commercial flight, passengers played second fiddle to the US mail. When travelers could book a flight, say, from San Francisco to New York, they would have to bundle up with extra clothing because no heat was provided. They could be bumped for additional mail at an intermediate stop, and, if they made it as far as Chicago, they probably had a plane or airline change. If they made it straight through without any problems, their trip took two days. Airfares in the early days were about the same as they are now in US dollars. Adjusting for inflation, that would make a one-way 1993 San Francisco to New York fare about $16,800. Commercial flight was obtainable only by the very rich.

The pioneer aircraft builders were truly entrepreneurs. With their own money and a small staff located in a barn or garage, they

Eddie Stinson was a hard-drinking, hard-spending barnstormer and quite a successful airplane manufacturer. His daring exploits with race car driver Barney Oldfield involved racing the car around a track with Stinson's Horace Keane Ace biplane. Stinson wanted to make these shows more exciting by landing inside the infield of the track. He moved his main landing gear forward, installed Harley-Davidson motorcycle brakes (the first brakes on an airplane) and accomplished the infield landings time and time again. American Airlines used the Stinson Reliant to do route surveys. This Stinson SM-1 Detroiter high wing monoplane is restored in Northwest colors. The SM-1 Detroiter made its maiden flight in 1927 and was placed into service with Paul R. Braniff, Incorporated, on 20 June 1928. It held five passengers and was powered by a 300hp Wright Whirlwind radial engine. The wingspan was 45ft, 10in, the fuselage was 32ft long. *Lawrence S. Smalley*

The Hamilton Metalplane bears a slight resemblance to the Ford Tri-Motor. Designed by James S. McDonnell in 1926, the type was manufactured by the Hamilton Aero Manufacturing Company. It entered service with Northwest on 1 September 1928. It was used in the first (that's right, it *wasn't* TWA) air/rail combination transcontinental services. Northwest fitted these and its Wacos with skis to provide service to snowbelt communities during the winter. The span was 54ft, 5in, the length was 34ft, 8in, with power provided by a 525hp Hornet radial engine. Northwest sold its Hamilton Metalplanes to Reeve Aleutian in December 1941. *Thompson Productions*

would design, build, and usually test fly their own airplanes. It was a time before wind tunnels; few rules of aeronautics were in print.

Wilbur and Orville Wright were avid readers. They studied the hang gliding experiments of Germany's Otto Lilienthal and observed the flights of birds. They read of the early 1800s aviation efforts of Sir George Cay-ley, whose plans included drawings resembling the modern airplane, and the 1842 plans of William Samuel Henson, who invented a device he called an aerial steam carriage. Henson's carriage was a monoplane with a tricycle landing gear and horizontal and vertical stabilizers.

On 30 May 1899, the Wright brothers contacted Samuel P. Langley of the Smithsonian

Institution. Langley had been studying aeronautics and supplied the Wrights with information, including a list of applicable books. To their surprise, the Wrights found that almost everything that had been published about the rules of aeronautics was incorrect.

Accidents were common. Amazing as it may seem, by 1912 there were 2,480 people with pilot's certificates worldwide and, up to 1910, only seven people had died from aviation accidents. Then, in 1910 alone, thirty-two people were killed in crashes.

There were two early Ford Tri-Motor types, the 4AT and 5AT. Shown here is the example from the Harrah's Automobile Collection in Reno, Nevada. Bill Harrah, owner of the Harrah's Casinos, was indeed a lucky man. He had the money to buy expensive toys like the Ford Tri-Motor and in his twilight years married a young country singer. The marriage didn't last, but the collection did. This ramp shot of the Harrah's TAT Ford Tri-Motor shows well its clean, well-polished metal surfaces and the historically accurate paint scheme. *Lawrence S. Smalley*

American Airlines used this restored Ford Tri-Motor at the delivery ceremony for its first Boeing 727-23. It then made a tour of the American Airlines stations in the US. This take-off shot is unique in that there is nothing in the photo to give away the actual year the photographer captured her on Kodachrome. *Lawrence S. Smalley*

## Aviation Heroes

There were heroes, too; many not recognized, a few famous. It seems that when we read a history of almost any of the pioneering airlines in the US, one name stands above the rest: Charles Augustus Lindbergh. His solo transatlantic flight of 20-21 May 1927, did more to awaken the world to the vast possibilities of airplanes being used for something other than war and mail delivery than all previous aviation milestones. It was Lindbergh's pure luck and detailed planning that made that flight successful; many had died trying.

Lindbergh's name appears in the histories of several early airlines. That may lead many to think that he couldn't hold a job. When further researched, however, one finds that it is a series of mergers and breakups of early carriers that account for his many employers. To many, Lindbergh is known more for the kidnapping and murder of his infant son than for his aeronautical accomplishments. In 1974, approaching death from cancer, Lindbergh flew to Maui to live out his final days. The captain of the United 747-122 asked Lindbergh if he would like to circle Maui, the island he loved so much, before landing at Honolulu. Lindbergh's answer was a kind "no thank you"; he didn't want to inconvenience the other passengers.

Ah yes, yet another aviation hero, Captain Eddie! Known perhaps more for his sharp tongue than his World War I exploits. Most of his statements about competitors of his Eastern Air Lines cannot be printed here. Edward Vernon Rickenbacker was determined and strong-willed, a fierce competitor. He reigned as the president of Eastern Air Lines from 1938 to 1963.

On 31 March 1931 commercial aviation was changed forever. Knute Rockne, a Norwegian-born American football coach at the University of Notre Dame, was one of six passengers killed when the Transcontinental and Western Air (TWA) Fokker F-10 in which he was a passenger broke up in heavy turbulence over Kansas.

Had there not been a celebrity on board that flight, the public might not have become aware of the crash. The plywood wings, thought to have been the cause of the accident, had been difficult to inspect. The only way to properly inspect the wing spars was to remove the plywood skins. Fearing a lack of confidence by the public following the crash, TWA wanted a metal transport with two or three engines capable of night flying. When they went to Boeing to buy the 247, however, they found that United Airlines had taken all delivery positions for several years. Finding themselves effectively locked out of the 247 market, TWA asked Douglas to build a metal airliner capable of maintaining level flight on a single engine and capable of night flying. The result was the DC-1, followed by DC-2 and DC-3 deliveries.

Well, it looks like pride came before parasite drag in the early days. This humongous metal plaque on the side of an Island Airlines Ford Tri-Motor probably cost a couple of knots airspeed and a higher fuel burn. *Gerald Modrak*

## Radial Engines

To the best of my knowledge, round motors or radial engines are unique to the air transportation industry. From the earliest radials to the largest and most complicated ones, they share some traits. One is a master rod that is cast as a part of the crankshaft on each row; each of the remaining pistons has a connecting rod with pins in both the piston and the crankshaft ends. If you are changing a cylinder and happen to let the master rod drop, you'll end up with some other piston rings dropping below the cylinder walls. Needless to say, a real mess.

While many people think radial engines are slow starting, there is a good reason they don't light off immediately. These engines have a dry sump—that is, an oil tank at some point in the nacelle other than below the crankshaft. Even during a brief through-station stop, enough oil can drip into a lower cylinder to cause a hydraulic lock. This can break the cylinder right off the aluminum engine case. For this reason during starting the pilot or flight engineer will count enough prop blades to assure two complete revolutions of the engine before turning on the magneto switches. Radial engines also have an odd number of cylinders in each row, usually seven or nine, though I have seen three and five on single-row engines.

Aircraft piston engines have at least two magnetos that produce their own electricity and spark; a battery is not necessary on the simplest of aircraft. Each cylinder has two spark plugs powered by different magnetos. On the DC-3/C-47, the two magnetos have plug wires going directly to the cylinders. The front plugs of both cylinder rows will be fired by one mag, the rear plugs of both rows by the other. Unlike automotive engines, aircraft engines were designed to be operated at idle or at a steady rpm in the 1900-2500rpm range.

This Ford Tri-Motor cockpit shot could have been right from the twenties were it not for the late-fifties invention—the Dymo Tape Label—on the panel. *Thompson Productions*

Because of all the pull of the propellers aircraft engines have thrust bearings to prevent the crankshaft from being pulled out of the engine. There is no vacuum advance but many aircraft engines have at least one magneto with a spring impulse coupling. This fires a delayed spark a little hotter and more delayed than normal. After the engine lights off, the impulse coupling will not work. On later aircraft, the magnetos supply voltage to distributors. When you shut down a piston engine, it should be done by cutting off the fuel or mixture. The magnetos are hot until the switch is turned off; that shorts out the magnetos. Power checks before takeoff are done on both mags, the left mag, back to both, then the right mag, and back to both. Only a certain predetermined rpm drop is allowed on one magneto.

On more powerful piston aircraft, there will be an oscilloscope in the cockpit from which a seasoned flight engineer can tell exactly which spark plug out of a possible seventy-two (in one engine) is not firing. My own experience as a student found this overwhelming and confusing. Engine shutdowns in flight used to be commonplace, quite unlike today, when an airline captain may go twenty years without an in-flight shutdown.

The most famous Lockheed Vega is the *Winnie Mae* in which Wiley Post and William Penn (Will) Rogers met their maker in 1935. The example shown here made many air show appearances and carried passengers at those shows in the mid-sixties. *Lawrence S. Smalley*

The Boeing 80A was used on Boeing Air Transport's San Francisco to Chicago service. Its first flight was in August 1928. The first revenue service flight was on 15 May 1930. A total of twelve Boeing 80As were built. The aircraft's wingspan was 80ft, and the fuselage length was 56ft, 6in. The first stewardesses were assigned to this equipment. Of particular interest is the airplane shown here in the Museum of Flight on Seattle's Boeing Field. When this aircraft was being disassembled for restoration, it was discovered that one of the three bolts used to hold the tail onto the airplane was missing. Using the latest in nondestructive testing equipment, it was determined that there had never been a bolt installed in that hole. *Greg Drawbaugh*

This restored Pennsylvania Central Stinson A is parked
at the passenger terminal building of Bowman Field,
Louisville, Kentucky. *David Potter*

In 1974, approaching death from cancer, Charles Lindbergh flew to Maui
to live out his final days. The captain of the flight asked Lindbergh if he
would like to circle Maui, the island he loved so much, before landing at
Honolulu. Lindbergh's answer was a kind "no thank you"; he didn't want
to inconvenience the other passengers.

O n 31 March 1931 commercial aviation was changed forever. Knute Rockne, a legendary football coach at the University of Notre Dame, was one of six passengers killed when the Transcontinental and Western Air (TWA) Fokker F-10 in which he was a passenger broke up in heavy turbulence. Had there not been a celebrity on board that flight, the public might not have become aware of the crash. Fearing a lack of confidence by the public following the crash, TWA wanted a metal transport with two or three engines capable of flying at night. TWA eventually turned to Douglas, and the result was the DC-1, followed by DC-2 and DC-3 deliveries.

Several North American Carriers used the Fairchild 71. This beautifully restored aircraft sports the early colors of Pan American. *Lawrence S. Smalley*

This Sierra Aviation Vultee V-1 was still airworthy when photographed in 1957. *Lawrence S. Smalley*

The Boeing 247 has been described by some as the first modern commercial airliner. Boeing Air Transport, forerunner of today's United Air Lines, placed it into service with a first flight on 8 February 1933. Their order for sixty Boeing 247s tied up production for years and thus limited the plane's success. That actually led to the development of the Douglas DC-1/DC-2/DC-3 series. The Boeing 247 had a wingspan of 74ft, a length of 51ft, 4in, and a maximum weight of 12,650lb. Its power came from two 550hp Pratt & Whitney Wasp radial engines. The example shown here is being restored at Paine Field, Everett, Washington, by volunteer Boeing craftsmen. *Joe Walker*

A Douglas Amphibian? You bet! The Douglas Dolphin was an amphibious version of the Sinbad flying boat. Only four were built for airline service, two for Pan American's C.N.A.C. operation in China, and two for Wilmington-Catalina ferry service. William E. Boeing (yes, that Boeing of Seattle) acquired one as his personal plane. The most notable fact about the Dolphin is that it was the first Douglas airplane manufactured for use as a passenger transport. The Dolphin had a wingspan of 60ft, a length of 45ft, and power was provided by two Pratt & Whitney R-985 radial engines. This example was caught on film at Sausalito, California, on 11 November 1961.
*Lawrence S. Smalley*

There was only one Douglas DC-1. It was developed for TWA and first flew on 1 August 1933. Seeing the outstanding performance and durability of the DC-1, TWA placed orders for the 2ft longer production version that would be called the DC-2. After a first flight of 11 May 1934, the TWA DC-2 entered service on the Columbus–Pittsburgh–Newark route on 18 May 1934, and the New York–Chicago–Kansas City–Albuquerque–Los Angeles route on 1 August 1934. Most DC-2s were powered by two Wright R1820 Cyclones. The wingspan was 85ft, and the fuselage length was 61ft, 11in. The magnificently restored DC-2 shown currently calls Long Beach, California, its home. *Brian K. Gore*

The Consolidated PBY Model 28 Catalina made its first flight on 15 March 1935. It saw extensive use during World War II and today is in demand as a fire fighting and sport airplane. During the war, Qantas operated what was then the world's longest distance nonstop flight between Perth and Colombo right under the noses of the Japanese Imperial Navy. The Consolidated PBY shown is in the late sixties scheme of Alaska Air Lines with Geoterrex titles. *John Stewart*

The Martin M-130 was built for Pan American World Airways. The name *China Clipper* applied to the first aircraft that made its first flight on 30 December 1934. There were only three such aircraft; the second was named *Philippine Clipper,* and the third was the *Hawaii Clipper*. All three were lost. *Hawaii Clipper* disappeared between Guam and Manilla 28 July 1938. *Philippine Clipper* flew into a mountain, 100mi off course, at Boonville, California, in 1943. *China Clipper* was destroyed in a landing accident at Port of Spain, Trinidad, 1 July 1945. Power was provided by four Pratt & Whitney R1830 Twin Wasps. *Thompson Productions*

The Sikorsky S-43 *Baby Clipper* flew in late 1935 with all thirteen airplanes destined for Pan American World Airways or its related companies, *Panair do Brasil* and *Panagra*. By 1947, seven had crashed. Shown here is Avalon Air Transport's N326 taxiing out from Long Beach Airport in August 1958. *Mel Lawrence*

On more powerful piston aircraft, there will be an oscilloscope in the cockpit from which a seasoned flight engineer can tell exactly which spark plug out of a possible seventy-two (in one engine) is not firing. My own experience as a student found this overwhelming and confusing.

Tail draggers can be challenging to even the most experienced pilots; ground looping and standing on the props are prime examples of those challenges. This Delta incident happened at Chicago's Midway Airport in the early fifties. The firefighters lassoed the tail wheel and pulled. It seems that no one anticipated how quickly it would fall. In a series of photos shot after the mishap, the last slide (not shown) shows a blur of the tail falling and firefighters running out from under it. *Gerald Modrak*

American Airlines liked and bought the DC-2 but wanted something better. What evolved was the DC-3 and DST (Douglas Sleeper Transport). American's DC-3s had Wright Cyclone R1820 single-row radial engines and a right-hand passenger door. An unusually sunny 4 July 1943 found this TWA DC-3 on static display at San Francisco International Airport's public open house. The slogan on the fuselage is indicative of the strong public support of our troops during World War II. *Paul White*

Douglas had made a prototype three-tail, four-engine DC-4E that never went into production. The design was scaled down by 25 percent to become the highly successful DC-4/C-54. There was no prototype DC-4; the first one was a production model. The first flight was 14 February 1942, and as the war was on all DC-4 production was switched to the military C-54 version. After the war, production continued with the last DC-4 going to South African Airways on 9 August 1947. National flew the DC-4 in the "Route of the Buccaneers" and "Airline of the Stars" paint schemes. This one, wearing the latter colors, is seen at Boston. *Ira T. Ward*

Capital wanted the public to think that its DC-4s were newer than they actually were. To give the impression of DC-6s, they painted black rectangles around the round windows. Eastern's Rickenbacker quipped, "Yeah. Next thing they'll be painting faces in the windows to make you think they're carrying people." A Capital DC-4 is shown at a Florida airport in 1957. *Thompson Productions*

The Boeing 314 made its first flight 7 June 1938. It entered service with Pan American World Airways as the *Dixie Clipper* on 28 June 1939. Twelve were built for Pan American. The first six were 314 standards; the last six were 314As with more powerful engines and were delivered later. The 314s were later brought up to 314A standards. Three Pan Am ships went to BOAC, and the US Army Air Forces used the 314 as a C-98 during World War II. None were saved for museums. A co-worker of mine at TWA, the late George Bailey, had worked on the Pan Am 314As as a flight mechanic and told tales of the maintenance tunnels in the wings that allowed access to the engines in flight. These tunnels were used more for repairing wing spar cracks than anything else and, according to George, it was quite common to be met in these tunnels by a slug of cold sea water upset by turbulence. The example shown rests in San Francisco Bay just off Treasure Island with the Bay Bridge in the background. *Thompson Productions*

I can remember it just like yesterday. During a lunch break at the Spartan School of Aeronautics in Tulsa in April 1964, I ran back to class to proudly tell everyone that I had just seen a four-engine C-46. Well... it wasn't. Next step, remove foot from mouth. I had seen a Boeing 307 Stratoliner. First flown on 31 December 1938, it was the first pressurized airliner. Pan Am took delivery of three, and TWA received five. Oliver F. Beech, my first TWA lead mechanic, told of the day in

December 1941 at the Intercontinental Division (ICD) at Wilmington, Delaware, when the US Army came in and gave employees a choice: stay there as part of the Army and work the 307s (now called C-75s), or be drafted into the infantry. After the war, TWA put on B-17G wings, engines, and tail surfaces and removed the pressurization. The photo shows a 307 of the French carrier *Airnautic. Via Robert A. Woodling*

*Left*
The Grumman G-21 Goose made its first flight on 30 May 1937. While they are still in service in fairly large numbers, most people recently became familiar with the Goose in the television series "Tales of the Gold Monkey." The examples shown are in the Avalon Harbor, Santa Catalina Island, in the colors of Catalina Air Lines. *Lawrence S. Smalley*

The Curtiss Commando C-46 was designed as the CW-20, a passenger plane with the fuselage constructed from two circular sections joined at the floor line. It was to have been pressurized. The twin-tailed prototype flew on 26 March 1940. Production models had a single tail and were not pressurized. This Northeast Airlines example shown at Boston in the mid-fifties is rare. *Richard J. Hurley*

W e've come a long way since 1903. Today, airline passengers think they have a problem if their individual video monitor or powered air vent doesn't work. In the earliest days of commercial flight, passengers played second fiddle to the US mail.

The Lockheed Twins reached their peak of development with the L-18 Lodestar. The evolution that started with the L-10 Electra eventually included the L-12 Electra Junior, with a first flight date of 27 June 1936, and the L-14 Super Electra, with a first flight of 27 July 1937. The Lodestar first flew on 21 September 1939, and in the US, National Airlines in Florida was the last major airline to have it in service as late as 1959. This airframe was modified extensively as an executive transport in the late fifties and early sixties. The photo shows a Pacific Alaska Airways L-18. *Pan American Archives*

The Grumman G-44 Widgeon first flew on 28 June 1940. It was much smaller than the Goose. This Interior Airways Widgeon was shot at Anchorage. *John Stewart*

The Vought-Sikorsky VS-44 was built for, but never taken by, the US Navy. Three were built and the first flight was 18 January 1942. One crashed in 1942, and American Export Lines used the remaining two on contract to the Navy from America to Portugal. The example shown here operated with Avalon Air Transport and later Catalina Air Lines between the Long Beach, California, seaplane harbor and Catalina Island. N41881 later went to Antilles Airboats, in whose hands the hull was damaged sufficiently so that the aircraft was no longer airworthy. A museum near Hartford, Connecticut, is now restoring it. *Thompson Productions*

Wilbur and Orville Wright were avid readers. They studied the hang gliding experiments of Germany's Otto Lilienthal and observed the flights of birds. They read of the early 1800s aviation efforts of Sir George Cayley, whose plans included drawings resembling the modern airplane, and the 1842 plans of William Samuel Henson, who invented a device he called an aerial steam carriage. Henson's carriage was a monoplane with a tricycle landing gear and horizontal and vertical stabilizers. On 30 May 1899, the Wright brothers contacted Samuel P. Langley of the Smithsonian Institution. Langley had been studying aeronautics and supplied the Wrights with information, including a list of applicable books. To their surprise, the Wrights found that almost everything that had been published about the rules of aeronautics was incorrect.

The Avro York was based on the Lancaster bomber with a rectangular fuselage. The first flight of the first of three prototypes was 5 July 1942. BOAC used the York first in passenger services, later in cargo services. Shown is a fixed display of a Dan-Air London Avro York. *Manuel Kolb*

# Chapter 2

# After the War

Immediately after World War II, aircraft manufacturers found themselves with great production capacity. They had the trained employees, wartime technology, and raw materials.

Lockheed brought back the Lockheed C-69 Constellations that the USAF had used and prepared them for airline service, a step that put them two years ahead of Douglas. By 1948, the Convair 240, Boeing 377 Stratocruiser, and Douglas DC-6 had joined the Constellations with 300mph pressurized cabin comfort. The Martin 2-0-2, though unpressurized, also entered service; it was followed by the 2-0-2A and the 4-0-4. Further improvements in engine and airframe technology saw giant strides in extended range and comfort. The DC-7C was the ultimate Douglas offering, but for long-range endurance nothing could match Lockheed's L-1649 Starliner Constellation.

There were problems, however. Both the DC-6 and the Constellations had problems with in-flight fires. The Martin 2-0-2 had a problem keeping its wings attached; the Martin 4-0-4 had an Achilles' heel in the form of remote compasses that would, on occasion, read 180° out. We don't seem to have such serious problems with aircraft introduced since the seventies. Maybe we've learned to ask what might go wrong instead of waiting for it to happen.

## First Fight Memories

My first flight was in 1949 on an American Airlines DC-3 from Louisville's Bowman

An Antilles Airboats Mallard. The Grumman G-73 Mallard, a bigger, modernized version of the Goose, made its first flight on 30 April 1946. Still in service in large numbers, some have been converted to turboprops. *David Howell*

A C-69 Constellation is shown on the ramp at San Francisco's old Bayshore Terminal in January 1951. *William T. Larkins*

In April 1939, Howard Hughes took the reigns at TWA. He and Jack Frye asked Lockheed to make a four-engine airliner for TWA and, in 1940, they placed an order for nine of the aircraft. (The order was later increased to forty aircraft.) The Lockheed C-69 Constellation made its first flight on 9 January 1943. Under the command of Howard Hughes and Jack Frye, the first production model completed a nonstop flight from Burbank, California, to Washington, D.C., in a record 7 hr, 3 min on 17 April 1944. Deliveries of the Lockheed C-69/L-049 Constellations began from Burbank soon after the war. Earlier versions had ground steering, which was accomplished through braking and engine power. That may have been all right in gate areas, but not for high speeds, especially where crosswinds or wet pavement was involved. Nosewheel steering was added. Note the old style "NC" registration of this TWA L-049 at Burbank prior to delivery. *Paul Xepoleas*

Field to Cincinnati's Sunken Lunken, now the site of Riverfront Stadium. Years later, I soloed from that same Bowman Field 3,500ft runway. Later in 1949, I flew from Miami to Havana and back. I remember little about both trips except that I was able to stand on the floor and look out the cabin windows that were just the right height.

I had been interested in railroads. My family for generations had worked for the Louisville and Nashville Railroad, but a 1960 trip to Europe and the various aircraft flown changed my life forever. I forgot about railroads and began to hang out at Louisville's Standiford Field (SDF). I spent what I could on flying lessons or a Lexington-Louisville Eastern Super G flight. Wow! Nine dollars for a first-class seat and the famous Golden Falcon Service!

For those who never experienced the sights, sounds, and smells of an airport in the fifties and early sixties, I regret that you will probably never really know what it was like. Oil dripped off the engines like dew in the morning. Gasoline was heavily leaded and color coded to indicate octane rating. Fuel trucks proudly displayed signs such as "145 Octane Aircraft Gasoline." Actually, octane tops out at 100. Numbers above 100 are performance numbers. Put this engine oil, lead from the fuel, lavatory fluid, and a hot, humid day all together, with just an observation deck or a 4ft high fence between you and the airplanes, and the smells would imprint onto your brain forever.

At the time, people still dressed up to travel. Men wore suits and fedora hats; women wore stylish dresses or suits with hats. Even children were forced into confor-mity despite their grumblings. Those travelers were a far cry from today's dress code, which seems to be dictated only by laws concerning indecent exposure. I look back on the fifties and sixties as "the good old days" and shudder to think what may happen in the future to make these last seven years of the twentieth century be called by that name.

TWA operated the L-749 Connies until 6 April 1967. Not all of them were in this paint scheme, which was intended to match the jet fleet. Too bad... The Super G or Jetstream L-1649 would have looked great in this scheme. *Harry Sievers*

A Capital L-049 at Miami. Capital started out with L-749 Connies but traded with BOAC for L-049s and cash. *Thompson Productions*

There were problems with some postwar aircraft. Both the DC-6 and the Constellations had problems with in-flight fires. The Martin 2-0-2 had a problem keeping its wings attached; the Martin 4-0-4 had an Achilles' heel in the form of remote compasses that would, on occasion, read 180° out.

Pan American Connies were delivered in the bare metal scheme but were later painted white. This example is at Boston in 1950. *Ira T. Ward*

Braniff operated two L-049 Constellations for a brief period. A cold winter's day at the Municipal Airport, Kansas City, Missouri, found this example at the extreme north end of the terminal next to the post office. The locals called this airport "Muni."
*Claude Thomas*

The Douglas DC-6 was the first real competition for the Constellation. First flown on 29 June 1946, American and United began regular flights on 27 April 1947. DC-6s were powered by Pratt & Whitney R2800 radial engines. The wingspan was 117ft, 6in, and the fuselage length was 100ft, 7in. Weather radar was not required until the sixties, so no airlines had it until then. It's 1966 as this then-twenty-year-old United DC-6 lands at Chicago's Midway Airport. The black window and door outlines were required by the FAA in that year. *Thompson Productions*

A Trans Canada DC-4M Mk2. The Canadair DC-4M Mark 1 first flew on 15 July 1946. Similar to a DC-4, the DC-4M had four Rolls-Royce Merlin V-12 engines. The later Mark 2 versions were similar to DC-6s with rectangular windows, pressurization, and the DC-6 wings, tail surfaces, and undercarriages. The transatlantic versions had Merlin 622 or Merlin 722 engines with three-blade props, while the domestic versions had Merlin 624 or Merlin 724 engines with four-blade props. Trans Canada, Canadian Pacific, and BOAC flew DC-4Ms. *Thompson Productions*

My first flight was in 1949 on an American Airlines DC-3 from Louisville's Bowman Field to Cincinnati's Sunken Lunken, now the site of Riverfront Stadium. Later in 1949, I flew from Miami to Havana and back. I remember just a little about both trips except that I was able to stand on the floor and look out the cabin windows that were just the right height. I had been interested in railroads, but a 1960 trip to Europe and the various aircraft flown changed my life forever. I forgot about railroads and began to hang out at Louisville's Standiford Field (SDF).

An American DC-6 on a layover in San Francisco in late September 1949. Considering what the automobile looked like in 1947, the DC-6 was like something out of the future. American used this paint scheme well into the jet years. The DC-6s were grounded after an American DC-6, N90741, landed safely at Gallup, New Mexico, with an in-flight fire. It was discovered that a fuel sump drain could leak and pour fuel directly into the cabin heater air inlet. This finding and an earlier fatal crash of United's DC-6 N37510 at Bryce Canyon, Utah, lead to the grounding of all DC-6s until March 1948. Of all the four-engine Douglas airliners, the DC-6/6B series were the most dependable and economical to operate. *William T. Larkins*

The Shorts Sandringham was derived from the military Sunderland. First flight was in the summer of 1946. There were twenty-one of all types built. The wingspan was 112ft, 9in, the length was 86ft, 3in, and power was provided by four Pratt & Whitney R-1830 Twin Wasp radial engines. Shown here is one of two Antilles Airboats versions that Charlie Blair, founder of Antilles Airboats, purchased from Ansett Flying Boats of Australia. His wife, actress Maureen O'Hara, accompanied him on the delivery flight from Sydney. Blair was killed while making an emergency landing with a Grumman in rough seas in the mid-1980s.
*Nigel P. Chalcraft*

An Albatross bearing the titles of Transocean Air Lines on their ramp at Oakland in August 1954. The Grumman Albatross was primarily a military airplane, and its first flight came on 30 April 1946.
*William T. Larkins*

Some airliners were produced in such small numbers that few people have ever seen them. The Douglas DC-5 is such an airplane; I have never seen a color slide or photo of one. Another rarity is the SAAB Scandia shown here. Many think it is a tricycle gear DC-3. The Scandia's first flight came on 22 June 1945, and only eighteen were built. Power was from two Pratt & Whitney R1803 radial engines, and this engine was never used on another type of aircraft. SAS took delivery of ten Scandias, and the remaining eight went to *Aerovias Brasiliano,* which became VASP. When SAS sold its Scandia fleet in late 1957, all went to VASP. The wingspan was 91ft, 10in, and the fuselage length 69ft, 11in. *Mel Lawrence*

For those who never experienced the sights, sounds, and smells of an airport in the fifties and early sixties, I regret that you will probably never really know what it was like. Oil dripped off the engines like dew in the morning. Gasoline was heavily leaded and color coded to indicate octane rating. Put this and a hot, humid day all together and the smells would imprint onto your brain forever.

The Martin 2-0-2 was promoted as the first postwar DC-3 replacement. The first flight was on 22 November 1946, and first service was in October 1947 with LAN Chile, and 15 November 1947 with Northwest. NC93044 lost its left outer wing in severe turbulence near Winona, Minnesota, and that led to the grounding of all 2-0-2s until late 1948. Northwest lost five more 2-0-2s before they were sold in 1951. Those incidents, along with the lack of pressurization, cost Martin many potential sales. Ex-Northwest N93045, California Central's City of Burbank, was photographed at SFO in late 1952. *William T. Larkins*

An American 240 around 1965 after weather radar was installed. Convair was the result of a merger between Consolidated and Vultee. The Convair 240 was the most successful DC-3 replacement (it was called the 240 because of its two engines and forty passengers). It made its first flight on 16 March 1947. Numerous innovations were added when building this airplane. It was pressurized by an engine-driven pneumatic pump mounted onto the accessory section of one of the Pratt & Whitney R2800 engines. To achieve a nacelle drag reduction, a torque nose on the engine placed the propeller almost 3ft forward of its mounting on other aircraft using the R2800. This permitted narrowing of the nacelle at the front. Instead of a ring cowl with numerous cowl flap shingles in a circle around the accessory section, there was a hinged, four-piece engine cowling that one mechanic with a strong back could open; the top and bottom segments had two cowl flaps each. The exhaust gasses passed through twin augmentation tubes that exited on the top trailing edge of the wing. Fresh air for the cabin passing through from the engine cowling through these tubes was heated by the exhaust gasses held inside the exhaust pipes. The augmentation system reduced drag, made the aircraft quieter, and added a minuscule amount of thrust. The wingspan was 91ft, 9in, and the fuselage length was 74ft, 8in. *Fred Erdman*

The Fairchild C-82 was a military transport used for airborne drops of soldiers and equipment. TWA bought one after the war. It was based at Orly Field in Paris and used for engine changes. The Westinghouse jet engine on the roof gave added speed. *Thompson Productions*

An Airspeed Ambassador of Dan-Air London. The Airspeed Ambassador, sometimes called the Elizabethan, made its first flight on 7 October 1947. Twenty were made, and they went to BEA. Power came from two Bristol Centaurus engines. The wingspan was 115ft, and the fuselage length 82ft. *Thompson Productions*

This is one of thousands of AN2s in Aeroflot colors. It seems that Aeroflot had at least ten different paint schemes on the AN2s at one time. At first glance, the Antonov AN2 probably does not look like an airliner. After all, it is used as a crop duster, trainer, and all-around military cargo and personnel transport. It could be fitted with floats, skis, or low-pressure tires, allowing it to land anywhere. After a first flight on 31 August 1947, more than 15,000 were made, and within the Eastern Bloc countries, AN2s seem to be everywhere. Powered by a 1,000hp ASH-621 radial engine, the AN2's upper wingspan is 59ft, 8in, and the lower wingspan is 46ft, 8 in. The fuselage length is 41ft, 9in. *Charles T. Robbins*

Cuba has nineteen AN2s registered to Cubana's
Aviacion Civil Division. This one has been heavily
modified for sightseeing with extra large cabin
windows like those of several Grand Canyon Twin
Otter operators. *Ruben Husberg*

# Chapter 3

# The Glory Years

The chapter title may bring a chuckle or grumble from anyone who was working as an aircraft mechanic in the forties or fifties. Imagine putting all your strength and weight onto a breaker bar trying to remove a spark plug and having the plug break loose quickly. Then imagine having all the skin peeled of your knuckles by the cylinder cooling fins and baffle plates. Or think about de-sludging a Hamilton Standard Hydromatic Propeller dome. The lead molecules that didn't foul the spark plug gaps seem to have all congregated inside the prop dome. It's slick aluminum on the outside, steel gears on the inside with a rubber piston seal that rides on the dome wall. When you finally got the dome off the prop, you probably had a fifty-fifty chance of it slipping out of your hands and landing on your toes. Even worse was trying to close all the engine cowling segments on a Super Con-nie after someone stole your "cowling stretcher," a 3ft long steel device allowing you to put several hundred pounds of force on the twist fasteners while pulling the cowls together.

Long-distance nonstop flights were becoming a reality in the late forties. Crossing the North Atlantic, passengers could hear the inflight crew cycling the propellers between

A Millardair of Canada R4D-8 in 1985. The Douglas Super DC-3 was different from the original version. While only five were made for civil use (three going to Capital), 100 were built for the US Navy as R4D-8s. The wingspan was 90ft, the length was 67ft, 9in, and there was a 39in stretch of the fuselage ahead of the wing. All tail surfaces were of a new design. The outboard wings were swept back slightly and new nacelles housed Wright R1820-C9-HE2 engines. Many ex-Navy aircraft are now being purchased by third-level freight and passenger carriers outside of the US. *Lawrence S. Smalley*

high and low pitch every hour or so to prevent the oil in the propeller domes from becoming so cold it could solidify and render the variable pitch inoperative. Those early flights needed more potable water capacity and more toilet waste storage. Passengers would become bored, there were no movies or stereo. There were no tray tables, your meal tray went on a pillow on your lap. With each meal, however, every passenger—including children—received a matchbook and a courtesy package of four cigarettes.

As more and more people of modest means wanted to fly to exotic places, some carriers began cramming as many seats as possible into airplanes designated for use in those tourist markets. When airplanes had mixed first and tourist class, the first-class

A United Stratocruiser at San Francisco. A massive airplane for its time, the Boeing 377 Stratocruiser was a civil version of the USAF KC-97/C-97 tanker/transport. The engine were massive four-row radial Pratt & Whitney R4360s that gave it a 4,200mi range at 340mph. Airlines could choose from rectangular or round cabin windows; some had both types, one on the main cabin level, another in the lower lounge. United's Stratocruisers had rectangular windows, and United's fleet was sold to BOAC in 1954. *William T. Larkins*

seats were in the rear. The reason was that from the leading edge of the wing to the cockpit bulkhead, the propellers mercilessly pounded on passengers' eardrums. When a prop blade shed ice, the noise could scare the hell out of anyone sitting near them. Just look at any photo of a well-used propliner and you'll notice a metal double skin on the fuselage in line with the props that looks like the roof of an automobile left outside during a hailstorm.

From the beginning of commercial air transportation and well into the nineties most airlines outside the US were government owned. The cabin interiors, from murals to carpets and upholstery, were representative of the national pride of each nation. Exterior paint schemes were complex and elaborate in some cases, such as Ethiopian Airlines and Eastern Airlines. Some were dull and unimaginative. Lufthansa, for example even today remains one of the world's "ho-hum" schemes.

As we moved closer and closer to the introduction of turboprop and pure jet aircraft, the technology available reached a pinnacle. Accidents were on the decline, public confidence soared, and more people began to fly. That, combined with the beginning of the interstate highway system in America, was bad news for the railroads. The railroads didn't lose much of the California to Hawaii traffic but took a real beating in markets such as Chicago to New York. Short haul markets such, as Los Angeles–San Francisco where there was an eight to ten hour drive on a lot

The cockpit of the same United Stratocruiser, which was hangared after the ramp photo was taken. Pan American was the first carrier to operate a revenue flight with the Stratocruiser. That was a San Francisco to Honolulu flight on 1 April 1949. As it taxied, a Stratocruiser typically left a trail of oil smoke, so it carried around fifty gallons of oil for each engine. *William T. Larkins*

of the two-lane US 101, saw the majority of travelers switching to the air.

If a person who had only flown in jets or turboprops were to fly on a DC-7, that passenger would probably be frightened by the shallow climb angle. A Delta DC-7 flight from Louisville to Atlanta in 1963 did that to me. It may have been a procedure to save engine maintenance (the Wrights to this day have a bad reputation for not liking large power increases, decreases, or long METO [maximum except takeoff] power settings) and not the abilities of the airplane. The DC-7 was faster than the Connies in level flight, but the Connies could climb steeply. As a result, point-to-point flight times were usually identical.

Like the plight of the wooden powerboats, the propliners were soon replaced by more modern turboprops and jets. The last time I went home with oil-soaked underwear and skinned knuckles, I swore I'd never work on a piston-powered airliner again. Now I miss them and long to work on them again.

Don't get me wrong, I'd like to work on one plane for one day only. The worst thing about being a mechanic on jets is getting Skydrol or jet fuel in your eyes. In those piston days, the hydraulics were Mil-Spec 5606, similar to today's automotive power steering or transmission fluid, and the gasoline didn't hurt as much as jet fuel. Well, enough reminiscing, let's look at airplanes.

Northwest's first 377 on a Boeing test flight. Northwest's Stratocruisers had rectangular windows on both decks. *Boeing Historical Archives*

Clipper Reindeer at Tokyo's Haneda Airport in 1957. The final Pan Am paint scheme for the Stratocruiser matched the soon-to-be-delivered jets. *Mel Lawrence*

Most of the Stratocruisers that were cut up for scrap met that fate at Oakland International Airport or Mohave Airport, both in California. I believe this photo was taken inside a BOAC Stratocruiser at Oakland. The view is looking aft from just over the wing. Note the stairway to the lower lounge, a divider, and the main cabin door. *Lawrence S. Smalley*

A freshly painted Ilyushin 14 awaits her next assignment. The IL14 first flew in 1950. Looking like a SAAB Scandia, it entered service with Aeroflot in 1954. Many are also found in Eastern Europe and China. *Thompson Productions*

An Eastern 4-0-4 in delivery colors. The Martin 4-0-4 was a great improvement over the earlier 2-0-2. The wing problems had been corrected and the cabin was pressurized. After a first flight of 21 October 1950, the 4-0-4 entered service with Eastern and TWA in 1952. Eastern took delivery of sixty, TWA received forty, and two went to the US Coast Guard. The entire production was delivered to US operators. Rickenbacker did not want the public to know that these were Martins because of the bad press with the 2-0-2s; he instructed his employees to refer to it only as "Eastern's Silver Falcon." Eastern never had a passenger fatality with its 4-0-4s but one did flip over on its back at Louisville's Standiford Field. *Ira T. Ward*

The Martin 4-0-4 exhibited an exaggerated nose-low attitude during approach and landing. One TWA captain told me it was the easiest-to-land transport he had ever flown. In his exact words, "You just aimed the nose of the airplane at the end of the runway." That landing attitude is shown in this photo of an Eastern 4-0-4 landing at Chicago's Midway Airport in the mid-fifties. *Mel Lawrence*

N40426 at Indianapolis Memorial Day 1958. TWA's Martin 4-0-4s were delivered with the fuselage painted white. They retained the same paint scheme and never had weather radar added until they were sold.
*Lawrence S. Smalley*

A Capital DC-6B at Midway. Capital Airlines leased some DC-6Bs from Pan American and introduced a new paint scheme in 1960. These were quickly returned to Pan Am as the United merger went into effect. *Richard J. Hurley*

The last time I went home with oil-soaked underwear and skinned knuckles, I swore I'd never work on a piston-powered airliner again.

The Brugeut 763 Sahara made its first flight on 20 July 1951. Sixteen were built for Air France, which used them from 1953-1971. I saw six of these at Orly in the early morning of 1 September 1961, and had no idea what they were, but they sure were ugly. Despite that, the airplane was versatile and economical to operate. Power came from four Pratt & Whitney R2800 twin-row radial engines. The wingspan was 141ft, and the fuselage length was 94ft, 11in. Shown is F-BASN. *Thompson Productions*

*Right*
A Western DC-6B at LAX in 1962. Western used its DC-6Bs into the sixties as "Skychief Service" against PSAs DC-4s, single DC-6B and, later, L-188 Electras in the heavily traveled San Diego–Los Angeles–San Francisco corridor. On my first trip to the West Coast in 1962, I recall seeing a sign at the corner of Sepulvida Boulevard and Imperial Highway advertising the LAX–SFO flight at $9.95 one way. *Jon Proctor*

A Convair Mainliner at San Francisco's old Bayshore Terminal. When Martin announced the 4-0-4, Convair saw it as a threat to its 240. Development of the Convair 340 began with a fuselage stretch 16in ahead of the wing to a total length of 38ft, and a wingspan increase to 105ft, 4in. Improvements were made in cabin pressurization, and more powerful engines were used. Delta and United were the first domestic carriers to order the 340. The first flight of the Convair 340 was on 5 October 1951. United's fleet of fifty-five Convair 340s operated its entire sixteen-year UAL service life without a passenger fatality.
*William T. Larkins*

*Left*
Shortly after the Dodgers professional baseball team moved from Brooklyn to Los Angeles, they replaced their Convair 440, which had been in a paint scheme just like Eastern's, with this DC-6B, N1R. The Dodgers used this registration later in the century with an L-188 Electra and a Boeing 720-023B, all registered N1R. Their DC-6B is shown here at San Francisco.
*Lawrence S. Smalley*

An early National Convair 340 was on a Boston
layover in the mid-fifties when this slide was shot.
*Ira T. Ward*

Long-distance nonstop flights were becoming a reality in the late forties. Crossing the North Atlantic, passengers could hear the flight crew cycling the propellers between high and low pitch every hour or so to prevent the oil in the propeller domes from becoming so cold it could solidify and render the variable pitch inoperative. Passengers would become bored, there were no movies or stereo. There were no tray tables, your meal tray went on a pillow on your lap. With each meal, however, every passenger—including children—received a matchbook and a courtesy package of four cigarettes.

This Braniff 340 was photographed at St. Louis' Lambert Field on 31 May 1964. The Convair 340 and 440 have integral airstairs in the left forward exit. The 240 had this on the right front or not at all when aft airstairs were installed. *Lawrence S. Smalley*

An American DC-7 on layover at San Francisco on 15 January 1959 (except for the radar nose there is little to give away the date). American Airlines went to Douglas with a demand for a transcontinental nonstop airplane. Douglas had to match the range of the turbo-compound Constellations if it was to remain competitive. Its answer was the Douglas DC-7 using the Wright R3350 turbo-compound engine. While the airplane reached the range goals, the engines proved unreliable. A contributing factor was the tight-fitting DC-6 type ring cowl that could not dissipate the heat buildup as well as the Constellation's cowling. After a few months' service, a large prop spinner was added to help a little. *Lawrence S. Smalley*

A Delta DC-7 taxies at Atlanta's Hartsfield International Airport in June 1967. For the novice, the easiest way to tell a DC-7 from a DC-6 is that the DC-7 has a four-blade prop, and the DC-6 series have a three-blade prop. The first flight of a DC-7 was on 18 May 1953. Delta was more satisfied with the DC-7 than other US carriers and kept theirs well into the late sixties. *Dean Slaybaugh Collection*

This striking photo of a Panagra (Pan American Grace) DC-7B shows how the wing looks without the saddle tanks. The DC-7B was developed in yet a further quest for increased nonstop range. It involved a stronger landing gear, more powerful engines, and, in the case of SAS and Pan American World Airways, saddle tanks for extra fuel, which were mounted on top of the wings aft of the engine accessory sections. *McDonnell Douglas Archives*

Eastern flew their DC-7Bs in three distinctively different paint schemes. N810D is shown here in the delivery colors at Midway. Note the Los Angeles Dodgers' Convair 440 at the far left in the background. *Mel Lawrence*

The second Eastern DC-7B scheme matched the Boeing 720 delivery. This example is at Dallas' Love Field in 1963. *Mel Lawrence*

National painted a few DC-7s in the DC-8 scheme; this aircraft was one of the last to get the older scheme. This fine-looking example at San Francisco parked next to the old American hangar on Christmas Day 1959 appears to have just come out of a D Check (airframe overhaul). *Lawrence S. Smalley*

As more and more people of modest means wanted to fly to exotic places, some carriers began cramming as many seats as possible into airplanes designated for use in those tourist markets. When airplanes had mixed first and tourist class, the first-class seats were in the rear. The reason was that from the leading edge of the wing to the cockpit bulkhead, the propellers mercilessly pounded on passengers' eardrums.

A TWA Super G on a layover at Chicago's O'Hare Airport in 1960. The Super G is perhaps the best known of the Constellation series. When the craft was fitted with tip tanks, TWA could fly nonstop transcontinental services in both directions. The first flight of a L1049G was on 17 December 1954. *Gerald Modrak*

A Super G at Idlewild in 1960. When this airplane was new, it bore the titles "Super G" with the "Fly Eastern Air Lines." Eastern continued to fly its Super Gs through 14 February 1968. That last flight was on the Newark–Washington National shuttle. *Thompson Productions*

Eastern wanted more Martin 4-0-4s but found that the production line could not be reactivated. Their solution was an order for twenty Convair 440s. Shown here is the Eastern Air Lines delivery scheme. *Thompson Productions*

From the beginning of commercial air transportation and well into the nineties most airlines outside the US were government owned. The cabin interiors . . . were representative of the national pride of each nation.

Convair had made further refinements to the 340 and named it the Convair 440. The most noticeable differences were a rectangular outlet for the exhaust augmentation tubes and, in most cases, a much bigger nose housing and weather radar antenna. Eastern's final scheme on the Convair 440s was the hockey stick shown here at Tampa. The left engine's propeller has been feathered, leading to a conclusion that there had been an in-flight shutdown, and, it appears they did not apply the tar first as the feathers didn't stick. *Bernard Schulte*

A DC-7C of Pan American World Airways. A 42in cabin stretch ahead of the wing, a taller vertical fin, and a 10ft wing extension of the Douglas DC-7B created the Douglas DC-7C. Pan American ordered the 7C so it could operate nonstop transatlantic flights in both directions regardless of the wind conditions. All DC-7Cs had saddle tanks. The first flight was on 20 December 1953. The Seven Seas' dimensions were a 127ft, 6in wingspan and fuselage length of 112ft, 3in. *Thompson Productions*

The Lockheed L-1049(A) was a stretch of the L-749. The shorter Connie fuselage was shaped like an airfoil. When stretched into the Super Constellation series, the stretch was accomplished both fore and aft of the wing with plugs joining those sections. The first L-1049 flew on 13 October 1950. The engines were not turbo-compound. Here is another Connie, a Flying Tigers Super H on approach to landing July 1966. The Lockheed L-1049H was designed to be converted between freighter and passenger configurations with minimal manpower and time expenditures. It was popular with supplemental carriers. The Flying Tiger Line probably had the most Super Hs. On my first day on the job with TWA, I helped hang the number one engine on a Tigers ship that had been in for overhaul. Tigers lost quite a few airplanes in that era; within the industry we called them "Falling Tigers."
*Thomas Kucherich*

A TWA L-1649. In my opinion, the finest piston airliner ever was the Lockheed L-1649. I remember two distinct experiences with this airplane. First, following my junior year in high school, I rode a TWA L-1649 from New York's Idlewild, International Airport to Shannon, Ireland, and on to Paris. It seemed to take forever. Second, while working at Kansas City, I walked from the overwing exits to the wing tip on the starboard side. The last 10ft was like a diving board. With normal steps it bounced about 2ft. On my knees crawling it still responded to the smallest move. The wing tips, to my surprise, were solid lead.
*Arthur Muhler*

Northwest and Braniff were the other major US carriers with the DC-7C. Northwest needed the range for its extensive Asian services launched from Seattle-Tacoma International Airport. Shown here is a

Northwest DC-7C at Tokyo's Haneda International Airport. With the Japan Air Lines DC-8 in the background, her days are numbered. *Mel Lawrence*

Foreign carriers also bought the L-1649, and here's a Lufthansa L-1649 at Tokyo's Haneda International Airport in 1960. New deliveries went to Air France, Lufthansa, Transcontinental SA (Argentina), and South African Airways. *Mel Lawrence*

*Right*
An Ansett of Australia ATL-98. The Carvair, or Aviation Traders ATL-98, was a conversion of the DC-4/C54. It had DC-7C type stabilizers and a cockpit in a hump over the main deck just like a 747. The first flight was 21 June 1961, and twenty-one were converted. Remarkably, though larger and heavier, the airplane had a better rate of climb than the original C-54. In the US, Aero Union, Falcon Airways, and Pacific Air Express have used the ATL-98. *Erik Bernhard*

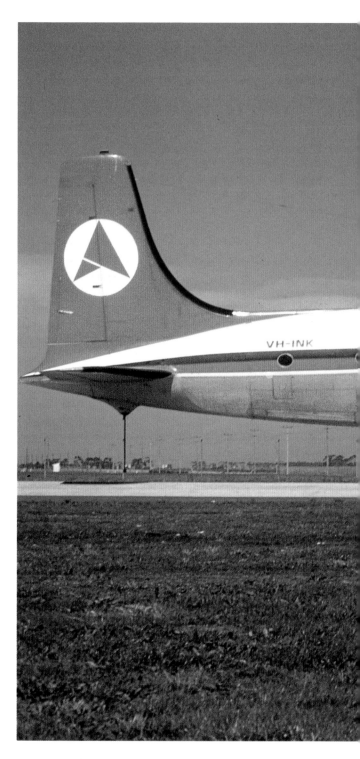

No DC-7s were manufactured as freighters; airlines had them converted. An American DC-7 Freighter lands at Oakland in the spring of 1962.
*William T. Larkins*

As we moved closer and closer to the introduction of turboprop and pure jet aircraft, the technology available reached a pinnacle. Accidents were on the decline, public confidence soared, and more people began to fly.

Eastern's L-1049G Super Constellations saw their last service on the Shuttle. Ship 239 lights off number two engine at Baltimore's Friendship International Airport on 1 November 1965. In a few months she would have her exit hatches and doors outlined by mandate of the FAA. *David W. Lucabaugh*

Eastern's first Martin 4-0-4 rests on an auxiliary ramp at Baltimore's Friendship International Airport on 15 December 1961. This is the Boeing 720-025 delivery paint scheme, and several bore these colors. I offered $500.00 for a slide of one of these and after five years it paid off. *David W. Lucabaugh*

If a person who had only flown in jets or turboprops were to fly on a DC-7, that passenger would probably be frightened by the shallow climb angle.

# Chapter 4

# Fall from Grace

In late 1958 and early 1959, the Boeing 707, Douglas DC-8, and DeHavilland Comet 4 began to take over the long-haul nonstops. Early in 1958, most piston-powered propeller transports had been in all-first-class configuration. Turboprops were being placed into service worldwide as medium- and long-range airliners such as the Vickers Viscount, Ilyushin 18, and Lockheed L-188 Electra began to replace Constellations, DC-6s, and DC-7s on the airlines' most prestigious routes. Modern piston airliners, the pride of the airlines just months earlier, were placed on shorter routes with multiple stops in small cities where they would have never flown before. Many piston airliners had their first-class accommodations ripped out and replaced with cramped tourist-class seats. As bad as that may have been for these once-proud flagships of the fleets, they would suf-

fer yet another blow in a few months as the turboprops were replaced on important routes with newly delivered Boeing 707s, Douglas DC-8s, and DeHavilland Comet 4s.

Third-level carriers (supplementals, or non-skeds as they were called) and even travel clubs were buying state-of-the-art propeller airliners to replace fleets of war surplus C-54s. Among the first to leave the major carriers' fleets was the DC-7 series. The Wright

The tired, old sayings go, "One picture is worth a thousand words," and "The handwriting is on the wall." Well, the TWA Boeing 707-131, bound for New York's Idlewild International and taking off across the Seaboard L-1049D at San Francisco International on the morning of 19 March 1960, showed the way of the future. Not only would the passenger carrying airlines receive more and more jets, Seaboard & Western, soon to become Seaboard World, already had DC-8 freighters on firm order from Douglas. *Lawrence S. Smalley*

Turbo-Compound engines, though almost identical to those on the Constellations, were stuffed into a tightly fitting nacelle. Engine overheating on the DC-7 types was a major problem. One of the most obvious attempts to fix the problem was a large, streamlined prop spinner placed over the Hamilton Standard hub. Another problem on the DC-7 was fuel burn. When the nonstop coast-to-coast capabilities of the DC-7 were no longer needed, American and United began to sell them off, Northwest converted some of its DC-7Cs to cargo configuration, and Delta and Eastern kept their DC-7s and DC-7Bs a little longer. In contrast, the DC-6/DC-6A/DC-6B airplanes were fuel-efficient. Their Pratt & Whitney R-2800 engines were more trouble-free.

The Convairs and Martins had a better fate than their four-engine cousins. Many local service carriers in America had begun to take delivery of the Fairchild F-27 turboprop in the late fifties but still had a number of DC-

Western's L-649A N86525 came from Pacific Northern Airlines via Chicago & Southern. With her sisters on a rare cloudy day at Las Vegas' McCarran Field in April 1, 1969, she awaits an uncertain fate.

The speedpak could hold 8,000lb of cargo from 55gal drums to large lumber products. It was raised into position under the belly with cables made into the speedpak. *Bernard Crocoll*

3/C-47 aircraft in their fleets. Pacific, Piedmont, Mohawk, Ozark, and Southern took Martin 4-0-4s from Eastern and TWA. Central, Frontier, Trans Texas, Mohawk, Lake Central, Ozark, and Allegheny also acquired Convair twins. In the seventies, Southeast Airlines used ex-TWA Martin 2-0-2As and 4-0-4s.

## Working on DC-3s and C-47s

Worldwide, the DC-3 and C-47 served well into the late sixties, and I worked on several of them. My first job after graduating from the Spartan School of Aeronautics in May 1965 was with Central Airlines at Fort Worth's Amon Carter Field (Greater Southwest International Airport—GSW). I also worked later at Kansas City Municipal Airport (MKC), called "Muni" by the people who worked there. Five nights a week, I worked the left engine of a DC-3 or C-47 by myself. That involved removing, cleaning, and reinstalling the Hamilton Standard Propeller Hydromatic Hub, the engine "cuno" oil filter, all the spark plugs, the ring cowl, and cowl flaps. I had never worked that hard in my life. It was a hard eight-hour graveyard shift. I'd go home at dawn drenched in so much engine oil that I would leave a dark oil ring on the toilet seat. My new bride found that disgusting.

The four-engine propliners also found a new career as fire bombers. Many of these airplanes that were used under contract with the US Forest Service to fight wild fires still bear their original airline registration num-

One of two Qantas C-54s rests at the northeast corner of Kingsford Smith airport. I ventured to Australia in February 1977 in an attempt to ride the last C-54 operating with a major line, Qantas. There were daily flights, I think to Johnston Island, but for me the destination didn't matter. What did matter is that I was there during the final two weeks of service with the C-54 and stood no chance of getting on board at an airline discount. For that matter, so many enthusiasts had come from around the world that I couldn't have even bought a full-fare ticket. *John Stewart*

bers and paint schemes with the titles and logos removed. Noted aviation photographer Bob Shane has devoted much time and effort to keeping a photographic record of these fire bombers, even to the point of going with firefighters into the fire lines to capture breathtaking action shots.

Some of the old piston propliners found final resting places at restaurants or cocktail lounges. It seems these can be found all around the world, from the Philippines to Australia, Europe, and America. Now, like a Broadway star who has found himself doing

A Transocean Stratocruiser in the airline's final days. As United and Pan American began to fly jets between California and Hawaii, Pan American did something that today could find them prosecuted for ruthless competition. Pan Am ordered first-generation jets from both Boeing and Douglas. They then advised both manufacturers that, should they sell jets to Transocean (a head-to-head competitor in that lucrative market) Pan Am would buy no more jets from them. Transocean held talks with American Airlines about leasing a 707-123, but that never came about. Left with Stratocruisers and Connies to compete against 707s and DC-8s, Transocean soon ran out of operating capital and shut down. *Lawrence S. Smalley*

summer road tours of *Death of a Salesman* just to keep a roof over his head, the once-proud major airline airplanes have found themselves doing local service, hauling freight.

The worst fate of all is the smelter. It deeply saddened me those first days on the job with Trans World Airlines at Kansas City International Airport (MCI) in 1966 to see a salvage operator using off-duty TWA mechanics to transform these magnificent machines into metal ingots that looked like big loaves of bread. The salvage foreman would paint zinc chromate cutting lines on the wings and fuselages with spray cans. The mechanics would then use chain saws (yes, chain saws!) to cut the planes apart. As one man sawed a jagged line across wing skins, control cables, and spars, another mechanic would stab that section with a forklift and dump it into the top of the smelter. I watched many TWA Connies and even a South Pacific Airlines Super Connie go to this cruel fate. Occasionally, a Connie would try one feeble attempt to extract revenge with small explosions as the chain saws entered a fuel tank that hadn't been completely emptied.

For nostalgia and the love of these once-proud airliners, many small groups have tried to buy and restore the propliners. Save-a-Connie in Kansas City has an L1049H and a Martin 4-0-4. The Mid-Atlantic Air Museum in Reading, Pennsylvania, has a Capital Vickers Viscount 700 and an Eastern Martin 4-0-4. Some planes, however, just couldn't be saved. The in-service loss of all three Martin M-130s was regrettable but not preventable. Sometimes, the extinction was just as senseless as

the extinction of plant and animal species. Case in point: the sinking of the last two Boeing 314s in New York Harbor, sunk by the US Coast Guard as a "hazard to navigation." They had been there for several months awaiting payment of fees to the Port Authority from their operator, World Airways. How I'd like to have one of these, the greatest of the flying boats, to live in, anchored somewhere in San Francisco Bay. I occasionally daydream about trying to locate and reflot one of the ships and fly it to California.

This chapter will show you what happened to many of our piston-powered propeller airliners. Some live on through conversion to turboprops or purchase by small carriers in the Third World, most have become beverage cans or cooking foil.

Slick Airways was primarily a cargo carrier. When the CL-44D swing tail freighters came on-line, the Connies were first to go. This ship survived to be restored by the Save-a-Connie Corporation. It is seen at San Francisco in early 1960. *Lawrence S. Smalley*

Convair twins began to show up in the fleets of local service carriers east of the Continental Divide. Shown is an ex-American CV-240 firing up. Note the mechanic crouched below the aircraft with the Hobart power unit. This aircraft was later converted to a Convair 600 with Rolls-Royce Dart engines and Dowty-Rotol propellers. Trans Texas Airlines was the subject of many jokes, the most often heard was that the TTA meant "Tree Top Airlines." Well, that little carrier became Texas International, then Texas Air Corporation, which bought Continental and Eastern. When I was working for Central Airlines in 1965, they had eight CV240s from American with Hamilton Standard propellers and two from Ethiopian with Curtiss Electric propellers. *Richard J. Hurley*

Ozark bought three "zero time" Convair 240s from a European carrier. Turns out "zero time" in the US means it is freshly overhauled. In Europe, however, it means no time left. The Convairs didn't stay long, Martin 4-0-4s from Mohawk replaced them.
*Lawrence S. Smalley*

A Convair 340 of Frontier Airlines at North Platte,
Nebraska, on 24 May 1964. United's CV-340s found
homes with several US carriers, but most retained their
UAL registration numbers. *Lawrence S. Smalley*

Braniff and Delta used the Curtiss Commando C-46 for cargo into the sixties. When the craft were disposed of, Braniff utilized the belly cargo space on its passenger planes, Delta replaced them with Lockheed L-100-10s which were converted into L-100-20s and eventually L-100-30s. *Thompson Productions*

An ex-TWA Martin 2-0-2A lands in Florida in the early seventies. The Martin 2-0-2A was an improved but still unpressurized version of the original. Here are a few pointers to tell a 2-0-2 from a 4-0-4: All 2-0-2s and the single 4-0-4 prototype have cockpit eyebrow windows. On the 2-0-2, the leading edge of the rudder trails off at the top; on the 4-0-4, the top of the rudder has a massive balance panel jutting forward at the top. The 4-0-4 has a cabin air intake for the pressurization system on the left lower fuselage. On the 2-0-2, the exterior door aft of the cockpit opens outward and slides forward; on the 4-0-4, it opens inward and slides forward. The most obvious difference is that the 4-0-4 has one more cabin window on each side. Because it was not pressurized, the Martin 2-0-2- series didn't last long. *Thompson Productions*

Left
Ozark's Martin 4-0-4s came from Mohawk, which had obtained them from Eastern. Ozark already had Fairchild F-27 prop-jets but the Martin filled a void and served well. This one was photographed at Chicago's O'Hare Airport. *Bill Thompson*

Southern used Martin 4-0-4s for sixteen years before replacing them with Metroliners. In 1978 several of my friends who are airline employees rode the final Southern Martin flight with numerous stops. Five of them moved from the front row seats to the rear row every few minutes, making the captain trim the airplane on the pitch axis. Finally, he came out of the cockpit and told them to knock it off or they would be deplaned at the next stop. *Dean Slaybaugh Collection*

The holes in the nose of this once proud BOAC Stratocruiser were punched with a forklift to facilitate ease of movement. To those of us who really love these old airplanes, that act is unspeakable. *Lawrence S. Smalley*

# Sources

The author extends his thanks and appreciation to the authors or publications listed here:

Cearley, Jr., George Walker, for the following books: *Braniff International Airways—The Building of a Major International Airline; The Delta Family History; Eastern Air Lines—An Illustrated History; Fly the Finest—Fly TWA; A Pictorial History of Air Line Service at Atlanta;* and *United—The Main Line Airway*

Cohen, Stan, *Wings to the Orient*

The Captain's Log, WAHS (March 1993)

Davis, John M.; Martin, Harold G.; and Whittle, John A., *Curtiss C46 Commando Flying* magazine, Volume 101, Number 3, September 1977, 50th Anniversary Edition

Davies, R.E.G., for the following books: *Airlines of the United States Since 1914; A History of the World's Airlines;* and *Pan Am, An Airline and its Aircraft*

Gradidge, J.M.G., *The Douglas DC-3 and its Predecessors*

Gunston, Bill, *Illustrated Encyclopedia of Propeller Airliners*

Hardy, M. J., *The Lockheed Constellation*

Harvey, Derek, *Seven Seas*

Ingalls, Douglas J., for the following books: *The Lockheed Story; The Plane that Changed the World;* and *The Tin Goose*

Killian, Gary L., *The Convair Twins*

Kruse, Richard, "Pan American—For 50 years America's Airline to the World," Journal of the AAHS (Winter 1973)

Macintosh, Ian, *Stratocruiser and C-97*

Marson, Peter, *Air Britain —The Constellation*

Mills, Stephen E., *A Pictorial History of Northwest Airlines*

Morgan, Len, *The Douglas DC-3*

Munson, Kenneth, *US Commercial Aircraft*

Serling, Robert, *Eagle*

St. John Turner, P., *Pictorial History of Pan American World Airways*

Taylor, Frank J., *High Horizons*

Woods, John and Maureen, *Constellation Production List*

Yenne, Bill, and Robert Redding, *Boeing, Plane Maker to the World*

# Index